...d on or before
...low.

SCIENCE Quest

SALT AND SAND SILVER

CONTENTS

MATERIALS

Objects are made from materials

Materials can be grouped in various ways – for example, according to whether they are metals, plastics or fabrics.

Group the objects in this picture into plastics, metals, textiles and pottery.

Look around your room. How many different materials can you see?

Why do you think so many different materials are used?

Most of the materials people use originally come from five main sources: the sea, the air, the earth, plants and animals.

Nitrogen is a gas which is used to make fertilizers. It can be extracted from the air.

Table salt is obtained from the sea or the Earth's crust.

Cotton is used to make clothes and comes from cotton plants.

What materials come from animals?

Materials which are found in nature such as wood, clay, cotton or milk are called **natural materials.** Some natural materials can be used just as they are. For example, wood can be used as a fuel or to build a log cabin.

Investigation

Dune grass

Aluminium comb

Cotton shorts

Steel can

Gold ring

Plastic straw

Polythene beach-ball

Alloy chair

Which of the above objects are made from synthetic materials?

SUMMARY
Materials can be grouped in many different ways.
Natural materials come from the sea, the air, the earth or from living things.
Synthetic materials are made by combining or changing natural materials, usually by a chemical process.

Most natural materials have to be changed in some way before they are useful to people. Some materials are not found in nature but are created from natural materials by chemical processes. These are called **synthetic materials.** For example, plastics don't occur in nature but are made from oil.

3

PROPERTIES OF MATERIALS
Choosing the right material

Different materials behave in different ways. For example, wood burns easily but steel doesn't. The behaviour and qualities of a material are called its **properties**. When choosing a material, the properties must be matched to the job which the material has to do.

Windows are made from glass because glass is **transparent**. Unfortunately glass breaks easily.

Bricks need to be strong enough to carry a lot of weight.

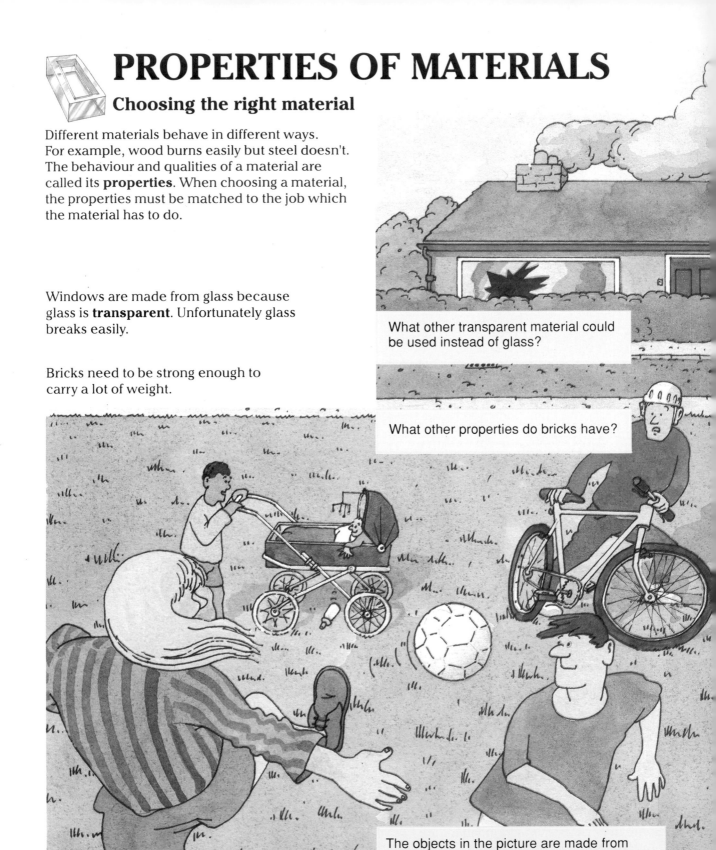

What other transparent material could be used instead of glass?

What other properties do bricks have?

The objects in the picture are made from different materials. Explain why the materials have been chosen to make the mountain bike frame, the football and the baby's bottle.

The frame for this slide is made from a material which is strong. The slide itself is made from a material which is smooth. The steps have a rough material on them.

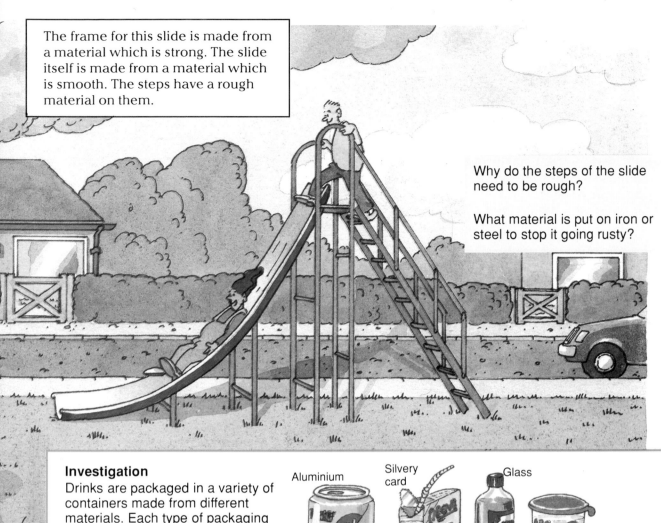

Why do the steps of the slide need to be rough?

What material is put on iron or steel to stop it going rusty?

Investigation

Drinks are packaged in a variety of containers made from different materials. Each type of packaging has different properties. The drinks inside also have different properties.

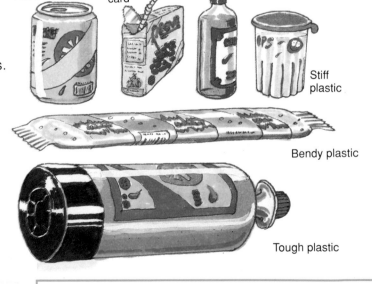

Aluminium

Silvery card

Glass

Stiff plastic

Bendy plastic

Tough plastic

Waxy cardboard

Why aren't fizzy drinks packaged in cardboard cartons?

Why is bendy plastic used for frozen drinks?

Why aren't soft drinks packaged in iron cans?

SUMMARY

Different materials have different properties. The properties of materials are matched to their uses.
Sometimes different materials can be used for the same job.

PLASTICS
Some synthetic materials

There are many different **plastics** and they have many different properties. Before plastics were invented, the word plastic was used to describe any material which could easily be moulded or shaped by pressure or heat.

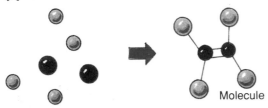

Molecule

All materials are made of particles called **molecules.** When plastics are made, small molecules called **monomers** are joined together to make long molecules called **polymers.** Plastics are polymers.

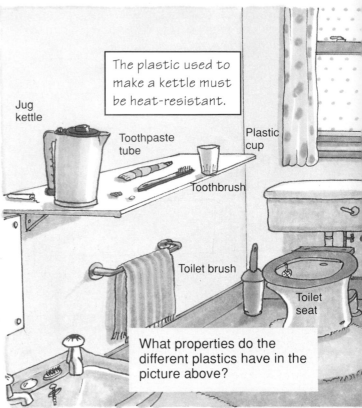

Jug kettle

The plastic used to make a kettle must be heat-resistant.

Toothpaste tube

Plastic cup

Toothbrush

Toilet brush

Toilet seat

What properties do the different plastics have in the picture above?

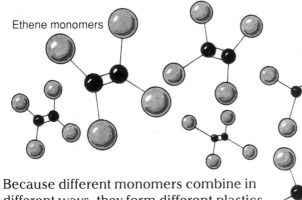

Ethene monomers

Polythene polymer

Because different monomers combine in different ways, they form different plastics. There are three main groups of plastics:

Mono means one. What do you think poly means?

Carrier bag (polythene)

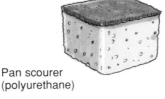

Pan scourer (polyurethane)

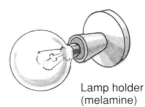

Lamp holder (melamine)

Thermoplastics
These soften when heated and are easy to mould and remould. They melt easily and are easily deformed by heat or pressure.

Elastomers
These are an elastic type of thermoplastic. They regain their shape after being crushed.

Thermosetting plastics
These can only be moulded once. After setting, they cannot be melted. They can be broken by crushing.

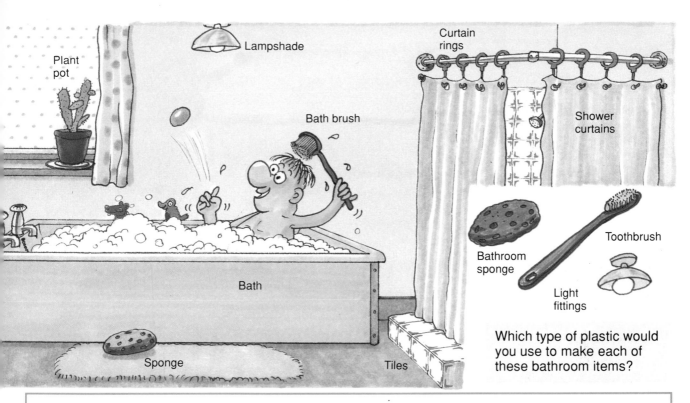

Plant pot

Lampshade

Curtain rings

Bath brush

Shower curtains

Bathroom sponge

Toothbrush

Light fittings

Bath

Sponge

Tiles

Which type of plastic would you use to make each of these bathroom items?

Investigation

Imagine you are in charge of a supermarket. It's your job to buy suitable plastic bags for use at the checkouts.

What properties should a plastic carrier bag have?

How could you test and compare the strengths of various types of bags?

Would it be a fair test if some of the bags had already been used?

SUMMARY

There are many different types of plastics and many different uses for them.

There are three main groups of plastics: thermoplastics, elastomers and thermosetting plastics.

Plastics are polymers which are long chains of molecules called monomers.

 # FIBRES

Using fibres to make textiles

Natural fibres are thin lengths of materials such as cotton, wool and silk. Cotton comes from cotton plants and most wool comes from sheep.

Synthetic fibres are produced from a liquid plastic such as nylon.

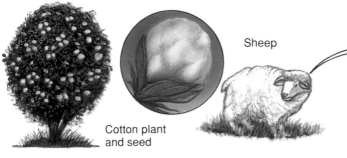

Cotton plant and seed

Sheep

Wool fibre

What sort of animal does silk come from?

Fibres are put together in many different ways to produce **textiles** or fabrics.

What objects in this picture are made from fibres?

Thin fibres have to be spun together to form yarn. Yarn can then be knitted or woven to make clothes, curtains and carpets.

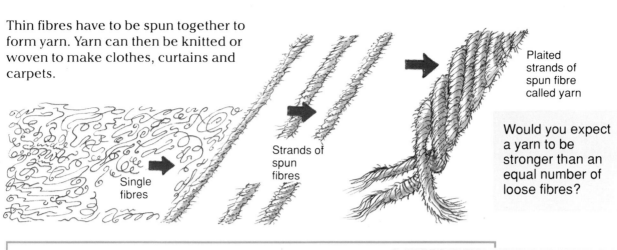

Single fibres

Strands of spun fibres

Plaited strands of spun fibre called yarn

Would you expect a yarn to be stronger than an equal number of loose fibres?

Investigation

When fibres are twisted together they trap pockets of air. Air is a poor **conductor** of heat, so fibrous clothes prevent loss of heat from the body and keep us warm.

Poor conductors of heat are called **insulators**.

Large air pockets

Yarn with trapped air

How do you think loft insulation helps retain the heat in a house?

Roll of loft insulation

A sleeping bag contains padding which insulates the person using it. Manufacturers give duvets and sleeping bags a TOG value which indicates how well they insulate.

Explain why different textiles may have different insulating properties.

Devise a fair test to compare the insulating properties of sleeping bags with different paddings.

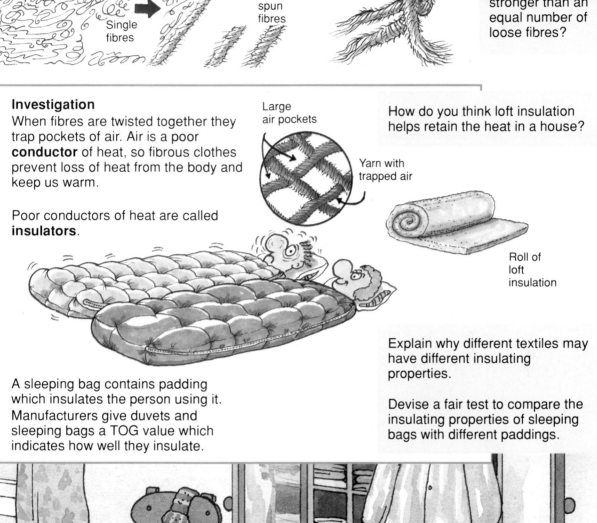

Describe some properties of each type of textile in the picture.

SUMMARY

There are two types of fibre – natural and synthetic.
Fibres are spun together to make yarn.
Yarn is woven or knitted to make textiles.
Textiles that trap a lot of air are good insulators.
Different textiles and fibres have different properties.

METALS

Their properties and composition

Metals are a group of materials which can usually be recognized by their appearance. They are normally shiny solids but they also have some less obvious properties.

Gold

Steel

Silver

What other metals can you name?

What metal is a liquid at room temperature?

Metals are **conductors** of heat and electricity. The lightning rod on this steeple is made of copper.

Many metals are **sonorous,** which means that they ring when struck. Church bells are often made of bronze.

Metals are **ductile** which means they can be drawn into thin strands.

Metals are **malleable,** which means that they are easily shaped. Lead is a metal which is soft and bendable. Sheets of lead are used on church roofs.

Lead conducts electricity. Suggest a reason why it is not used for lightning rods.

10

Investigation
The base of a cooking pan needs to be a good conductor of heat.

Cooking pans are made from a variety of metals.

Cast iron

Stainless steel

Aluminium

Steel and copper

Not all metals are suitable for cooking pans. Most metals **corrode**, or rust, when in contact with damp air.

What other properties must be considered when choosing a metal for making a pan?

There are about eighty naturally occurring metals. **Alloys** can be formed by combining metals with small amounts of other substances. Alloys have properties which natural metals do not. Steel is an alloy. It is mainly iron with a small amount of carbon. The carbon gives the alloy more strength and makes it harder. Other substances may be added to iron to make other types of steel.

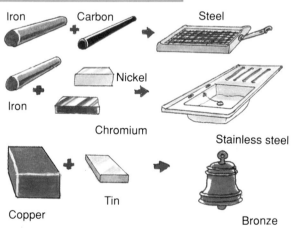

Iron + Carbon → Steel

Iron + Nickel, Chromium → Stainless steel

Copper + Tin → Bronze

What advantage does stainless steel have over ordinary steel?

Coins are made of metal alloys. What is an obvious difference between the alloys used to make these coins?

SUMMARY
Metals are good conductors of heat and electricity.
Metals are malleable, ductile and can be polished.
Metals are usually sonorous.
An alloy is a mixture of metals or a mixture of metals and other substances.

GLASS
Its properties and uses

There are many different types of glass. The most common is the type used for windows. This is made by mixing and heating sand (silicon dioxide), limestone (calcium carbonate) and soda-ash (sodium carbonate). Sometimes cullet (broken glass) is also added to the mixture. Chemicals called **metal oxides** may also be added to give the glass a colour.

Glass is a very stable material. It doesn't corrode and it isn't dissolved by water or most other chemicals. This means that it can be used to make containers for most liquids including food and drinks.

Green glass contains iron oxide.

Brown glass contains barium oxide.

What advantages and disadvanges are there in using glass as a drinks container?

The arrangement of particles in molten glass, like many other liquids, allows light to pass through. When the liquid glass is rapidly cooled, the particles in the glass lose their energy and almost stop moving. The particles stay in the position they had when the glass was liquid. 'Solid' glass is really a very thick liquid.

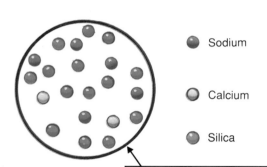

- Sodium
- Calcium
- Silica

This diagram represents the arrangement of particles in a piece of glass.

Molten gas can be extruded into long fibres. The fibres are used to make loft insulation and fibre-glass items such as canoes.

Where is glass being used in this picture?

Glass is very brittle. That means it won't bend much without breaking. Rapid heating and cooling also breaks glass.

Because broken glass is dangerous, stronger glass is produced for some purposes.

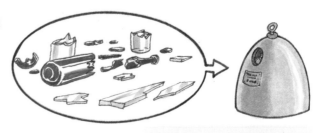

How is broken glass useful?

Toughened glass
This is used for the side windows of cars. Its particles are arranged during its manufacture in such a way that, when broken, it shatters into tiny harmless pieces.

Ordinary glass
Toughened glass

Describe the difference in the arrangement of these particles.

Safety glass
This is used for car windscreens. It consists of two sheets of toughened glass with a thin layer of a plastic between them. The plastic holds the pieces of broken glass together if a stone hits the windscreen.

Glass
Plastic
Glass

Why is it safer for a driver if a windscreen stays in one piece after shattering?

Borosilicate glass
This is used in 'Pyrex' dishes and laboratory glassware. It contains boron, which makes it less likely to break during rapid heating and cooling.

Boron particle

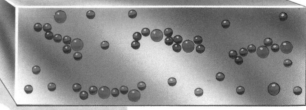

Borosilicates are polymers. What property of polymers helps give this sort of glass its properties?

SUMMARY
Glass is usually transparent.
Glass is coloured by adding chemicals called metal oxides.
Glass resists corrosion.
Glass can be toughened during its manufacture.
Safety glass is made from layers of toughened glass and plastic.

CERAMICS AND CLAY

The uses and properties of baked clay

Ceramics are formed by baking clay, which is a plentiful material found in the Earth's crust. Clay contains varying amounts of potassium, aluminium, silicon, oxygen and water and traces of other substances. Different clays produce different ceramics.

Toilet

Greek bowl

Brick

Some ceramic objects

What ceramic objects can you see in the picture below? What different properties do they have?

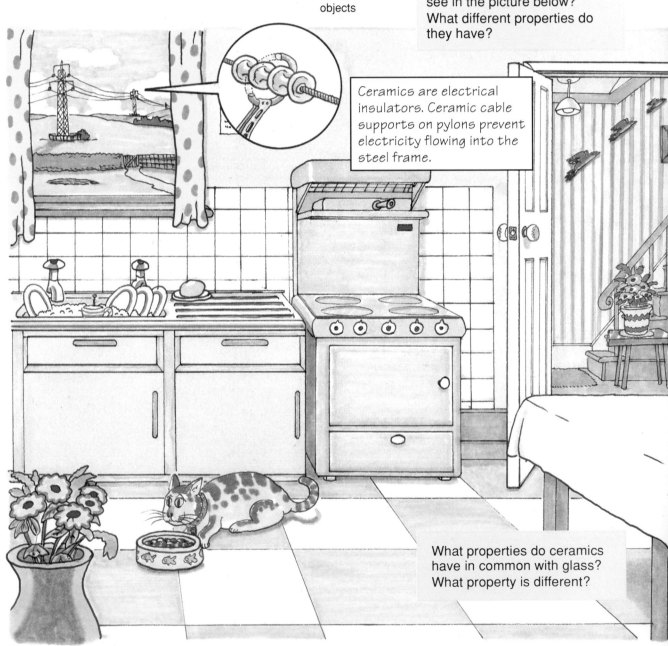

Ceramics are electrical insulators. Ceramic cable supports on pylons prevent electricity flowing into the steel frame.

What properties do ceramics have in common with glass? What property is different?

The molecules in clay tend to stick to each other in layers which are only one molecule thick. The water molecules in damp clay help one layer to slide over one another. This is why damp clay is easily shaped. The more water there is in a clay, the more malleable it is.

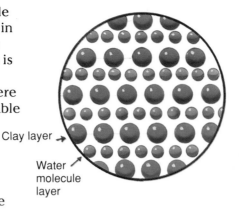

Clay layer →

Water molecule layer ↗

Shaping the clay

How will removing the water affect the properties of the clay?

After it has been shaped, the clay item is left at room temperature to dry out. This allows the water molecules to evaporate and the clay shrinks and becomes hard.

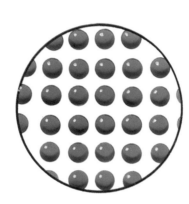

Drying out

What has happened to the clay layers?

Once the clay has dried, it is baked, or **fired**, in a **kiln** at up to 1700 °C. Most pottery begins to melt above this temperature. During the firing, the clay molecules move closer together and become fused. Once a pot has been fired, there is not enough room between the molecules for water to re-enter.

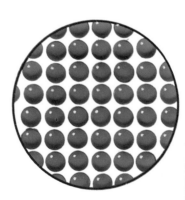

Fired pot

Explain why a ceramic vase doesn't become malleable when filled with water.

Explain why ceramics are brittle.

SUMMARY
Different ceramics have different properties.
Ceramics are electrical insulators.
Ceramics have a high melting point.
Ceramics are inert which means that they are not affected by contact with other chemicals.
Ceramics are hard but brittle.

15

CHEMICAL REACTIONS
How new substances are created

Many substances react with each other when they come into contact. Substances which don't react with other materials are called **inert.**

A **chemical reaction** is a process in which at least one substance is changed into another. For example, if a steel object is left in the rain, it becomes rusty.

Water and oxygen in the air react with the iron in the steel to produce a new substance – rust. This can be written as a **word equation** like this:

Iron + Oxygen + Water → Rust (hydrated iron oxide)

The substances which react together are called **reactants**. Any new substances produced are called **products.**

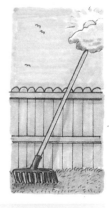

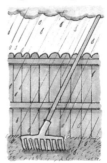

What substances have reacted to make this rake go rusty?

What are the reactants which are affecting the surface of this spade?

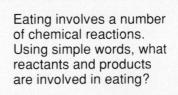

Eating involves a number of chemical reactions. Using simple words, what reactants and products are involved in eating?

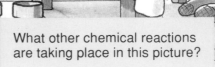

What other chemical reactions are taking place in this picture?

The simplest materials from which substances can be made are called **elements**. The smallest part of an element is called an **atom.** The atoms of one element are all the same but they are different from the atoms of all other elements. Atoms don't normally exist alone but instead join with other atoms to form **molecules**. For example, two atoms of oxygen combine to form a molecule of oxygen.

Two hydrogen atoms → Hydrogen molecule

When atoms of different elements combine, molecules of new substances are created. For example, two atoms of hydrogen combine with one atom of oxygen to make one molecule of water.

A molecule of rust is made up of two atoms of iron and three atoms of oxygen attached to a molecule of water.

Scientists use letters, numbers and symbols to show how chemicals react. The names of atoms are usually indicated by their first letter in capitals, sometimes followed by a second small letter. For example Fe is the symbol for iron (Ferrum is an old name for iron).

The **chemical equation** opposite says that four iron atoms combine with three oxygen molecules and a molecule of water to produce two molecules of rust (hydrated iron oxide).

The substances on the left of the arrow are the reactants and the substances on the right are the products.

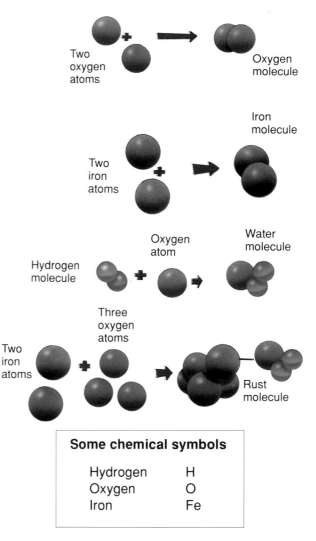

Two oxygen atoms → Oxygen molecule

Two iron atoms → Iron molecule

Hydrogen molecule + Oxygen atom → Water molecule

Two iron atoms + Three oxygen atoms → Rust molecule

Some chemical symbols

Hydrogen	H
Oxygen	O
Iron	Fe

$$4Fe + 3O_2 + H_2O \rightarrow 2Fe_2O_3 .H_2O$$

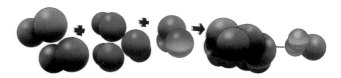

Rust molecule

What is the chemical formula for this rust molecule?

SUMMARY
In a chemical reaction, reactants come into contact and produce products.
Symbols are used to show what reactants are involved in a chemical reaction and what products are produced.
Numbers are used in equations to show the number of atoms and molecules involved.

REACTION SPEEDS
Factors affecting the rate of chemical reactions

All substances possess **chemical energy**. During a chemical reaction, energy may be released or taken in. If energy is released, an **exothermic reaction** takes place. If energy is taken in, an **endothermic reaction** takes place.

In a bonfire, wood reacts with oxygen to produce ashes and smoke. The chemical energy is released in the form of light, heat and sound.

Usually, some energy has to be supplied to the reactants to start off a reaction. This energy is called the **activation energy**.

The speed at which a reaction takes place depends on the readiness of the reactants to either combine or decompose. When something **decomposes** it breaks up into simpler substances. Adding heat often increases the speed of a reaction.

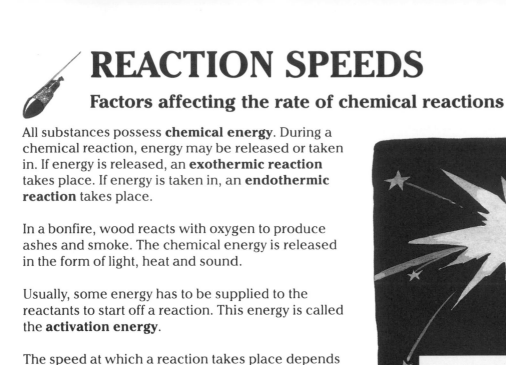

How is activation energy initially supplied to the chemicals in a rocket?

What reactions are taking place in this picture?

What forms of energy are being given off?

Does gunpowder or wood combine most readily with oxygen?

During a chemical reaction molecules in the reactants come into contact with each other. The more molecules in contact, the greater the speed of the reaction.

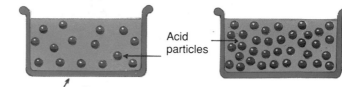

Acid particles

Hydrochloric acid

Which is the most concentrated of these two samples of hydrochloric acid?

Concentrated acid has more acid molecules than dilute acid.

If magnesium is added to hydrochloric acid, the reaction produces magnesium chloride and hydrogen gas. Adding heat makes the molecules more mobile and more of them come into contact during a given time.

Will concentrated or dilute hydrochloric acid produce the quickest reaction?

Will adding heat speed up or slow down the reaction?

Magnesium atom

Hydrochloric acid molecule

Collisions between magnesium atoms and hydrochloric acid molecules

Investigation

At room temperature, hydrogen peroxide slowly decomposes into water and oxygen. The reaction can be speeded up by using a **catalyst**. A catalyst is a substance which lowers the activation energy.

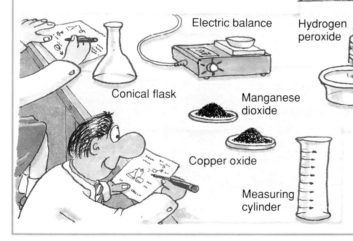

Electric balance

Hydrogen peroxide

Bowl

Conical flask

Manganese dioxide

Spatula

Timer

Copper oxide

Delivery tube

Measuring cylinder

Using the apparatus above, how would you find out which is the most effective catalyst?

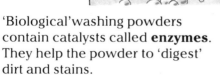

'Biological' washing powders contain catalysts called **enzymes**. They help the powder to 'digest' dirt and stains.

Do you think your body contains enzymes? Explain your answer.

SUMMARY

All substances contain chemical energy. Energy is released or taken in during a chemical reaction.

The speed of a reaction is affected by heat and the number of reactant molecules in contact.

Catalysts are used to speed up reactions. They work by lowering the activation energy.

REACTIVITY AND METALS

How metals tend to react

A metal **corrodes** when a chemical reacts with its surface. Water, air and acids are the most common of these corrosive chemicals.

The reactivity series is a sort of league table of the **reactivity** of metals. Potassium is near the top. It is very reactive and burns on contact with cold water.

Rust forms slowly on iron. Iron is near the middle of the reactivity series.

Titanium is a light, strong metal used where only a small amount of corrosion is acceptable. It is used in aircraft construction and for artificial hip joints.

This table lists some metals in order of their reactivity
Potassium
Sodium
Calcium
Magnesium
Aluminium
Zinc
Iron
Tin
Lead
Copper
Mercury
Silver
Gold

Do you think titanium appears near the top or the bottom of the reactivity series? Explain your answer.

Artificial hip joint

A metal may be protected from corrosion by **electroplating.** This process coats the metal with another metal which appears below it in the reactivity series. For example, steel food cans are usually plated with tin. Some people have gold-plated taps. The metal used for the coating doesn't corrode as quickly as the metal which it protects.

Suggest another metal which could be used to coat iron buckets.

Iron with a coating of zinc is called **galvanized** iron. Zinc is more reactive than iron and soon corrodes to form zinc oxide. The zinc oxide is insoluble and protects the rest of the zinc and iron underneath from further corrosion.

Some metals, such as aluminium, may be **anodized** to reduce corrosion. The surface is coated with insoluble aluminium oxide. Metal dyes are often added to the oxides to give them a colour.

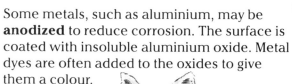

Why do you think drinks cans aren't coated with potassium?

Anodized name tag

Anodized area

Look around your room.
Where can you see examples of electroplating and galvanizing?

SUMMARY

The reactivity series table allows us to compare the reactivity of metals.

The most reactive metals are near the top.
The least reactive are near the bottom.

Metals can be protected from corrosion by electroplating, galvanizing and anodizing.

REACTIVITY AND ATOMS

Electron shells, ions and bonds

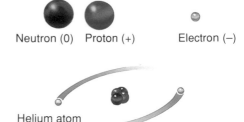

Neutron (0)   Proton (+)   Electron (−)

Atoms are made up of small particles called **protons, neutrons** and **electrons.** Neutrons have no charge, protons are positively charged and electrons are negatively charged. An atom is neutral because the opposite charges cancel each other out.

Protons and neutrons clump together in the centre, or **nucleus,** of the atom. Electrons orbit the nucleus. In a normal atom the number of electrons is equal to the number of protons.

Electrons orbit the nucleus at about 1000 km/hr. They constantly change direction but stay at the same distance from the nucleus. The orbit which an electron occupies is called a **shell.**

Atoms may possess more than one shell containing orbiting electrons. For example, helium has one shell of two electrons. Lithium has an inner shell of two electrons and an second shell containing one electron.

Electrons may occupy up to seven shells, one inside the other. Each shell contains one or more electrons.

Helium atom

A sodium atom has eleven protons. How many electrons does it have?

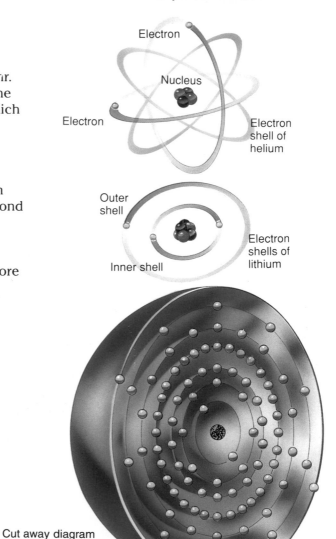

Electron

Nucleus

Electron

Electron shell of helium

Outer shell

Inner shell

Electron shells of lithium

Shell	Maximum number of electrons
First	2
Second	8
Third	18
Fourth	32

Cut away diagram of electron shells in thorium atom

Sodium has two electrons in the inner shell and eight electrons in the second shell. How many electrons does sodium have in its outer shell?

A sodium atom has one electron in its outer shell. A single electron tends to be only loosely attached to the rest of the atom. If this electron were to escape, the negative and positive charges would no longer be equal and the atom would become an ion.

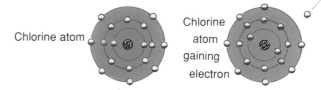

What would the charge be on the sodium ion after losing a negatively charged electron?

A chlorine atom has seven electrons in its outer shell. This arrangement tends to attract free electrons such as the one from the sodium atom. If an extra electron joins a chlorine atom, the negative and positive charges of this atom would no longer be equal.

What would the charge be on the chlorine ion after gaining a negatively charged electron?

An atom which has lost or gained one or more electrons is called an **ion**. After losing an electron, a sodium atom becomes a positive sodium ion. After gaining an electron, a chlorine atom becomes a negative chlorine ion.

Sodium ion(+)   Chlorine ion(−)

Positive and negative ions strongly attract each other. They join together and form a new chemical substance by **ionic bonding.**

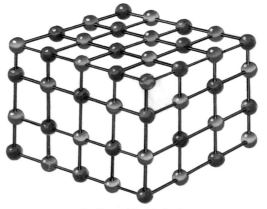

Equal numbers of sodium and chlorine ions bond together to form a regular pattern of ions called a **lattice.** The new substance is called sodium chloride or table salt.

All atoms and groups of atoms which become negative or positive ions can then bond with oppositely charged ions to form **ionic compounds.**

Sodium chloride lattice

Can lithium bond with chlorine? Explain your answer.

Would you expect potassium to be more reactive than sodium? Explain your answer.

SUMMARY
Atoms consist of protons, electrons and neutrons.
Electrons orbit the nucleus of atoms in shells.
Positive and negative ions attract each other.
Ionic bonding forms ionic compounds.

THE PERIODIC TABLE

Atomic numbers and properties of elements

An element is a pure substance which cannot be changed into a simpler substance by a chemical reaction.

There are 105 named elements. They all have different properties depending on how many atomic particles they contain. The **atomic number** of an element is the number of protons in an atom of the element. An atom may lose or gain electrons during a reaction but not neutrons or protons.

A small difference between atoms can make a big difference between the properties of elements.

Elements with atomic number 1 to 92 are naturally ocurring and the rest are synthetic.

Elements can be put into chemical groups according to their properties. For example group I elements have similar properties.

The elements in a **chemical group** always have the same number of electrons in the outer shell.

The **Periodic Table** of elements shown on page 25 indicates the relationship between the atomic numbers and the properties of elements.

Ernest Rutherford

The Periodic Table was devised by the Russian chemist Dmitri Mendeléev and improved by Henry Moseley and Ernest Rutherford.

There is an element with atoms having 11 protons and 12 neutrons in the nucleus.
What is its atomic number?

Neon is an inert gas with atomic number 10

Sodium is a reactive metal with atomic number 11

How do these two elements differ?

Some groups of elements have special names:

Group   I – alkali metals
Group   II – alkaline earth metals
Group VII – halogens
Group   0 – inert or noble gases

ALKALI METAL GROUP		
Name	**Atomic number**	**Electrons in shells**
Lithium	3	2, 1
Sodium	11	2, 8, 1
Potassium	19	2, 8, 8, 1
Rubidium	37	2, 8, 18, 1
Caesium	55	2, 8, 18, 18, 8, 1
Francium	87	2, 8, 18, 32, 18, 8, 1

The Periodic Table of the Elements

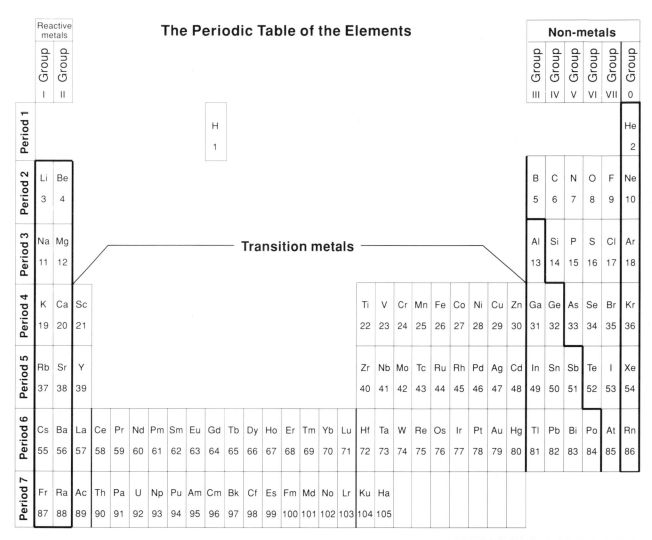

Reactive metals

	Group I	Group II																Group III	Group IV	Group V	Group VI	Group VII	Group 0
Period 1								H 1															He 2
Period 2	Li 3	Be 4																B 5	C 6	N 7	O 8	F 9	Ne 10
Period 3	Na 11	Mg 12					Transition metals											Al 13	Si 14	P 15	S 16	Cl 17	Ar 18
Period 4	K 19	Ca 20	Sc 21				Ti 22	V 23	Cr 24	Mn 25	Fe 26	Co 27	Ni 28	Cu 29	Zn 30	Ga 31	Ge 32	As 33	Se 34	Br 35	Kr 36
Period 5	Rb 37	Sr 38	Y 39				Zr 40	Nb 41	Mo 42	Tc 43	Ru 44	Rh 45	Pd 46	Ag 47	Cd 48	In 49	Sn 50	Sb 51	Te 52	I 53	Xe 54
Period 6	Cs 55	Ba 56	La 57	Ce 58	Pr 59	Nd 60	Pm 61	Sm 62	Eu 63	Gd 64	Tb 65	Dy 66	Ho 67	Er 68	Tm 69	Yb 70	Lu 71	Hf 72	Ta 73	W 74	Re 75	Os 76	Ir 77	Pt 78	Au 79	Hg 80	Tl 81	Pb 82	Bi 83	Po 84	At 85	Rn 86
Period 7	Fr 87	Ra 88	Ac 89	Th 90	Pa 91	U 92	Np 93	Pu 94	Am 95	Cm 96	Bk 97	Cf 98	Es 99	Fm 100	Md 101	No 102	Lr 103	Ku 104	Ha 105

Non-metals

Reading from left to right in a **period** (horizontal row), there is a gradual change from metallic to non-metallic elements. Alkali metals are said to be very metallic. Inert gases are said to be very non-metallic.

Where are the metals in the Periodic Table?

Where are the non-metals in the Periodic Table?

Which is the most metallic – sodium(Na), silicon(Si) or sulphur(S)?

SUMMARY
Elements cannot be changed into simpler substances by a chemical reaction.

Elements in a chemical group have similar properties and the same number of electrons in the outer shell.

A Periodic Table shows the relationship between the atomic numbers of elements and how metallic the elements are.

ACIDS AND ALKALIS

Definitions and tests for acids and alkalis

An **acid** is a substance which corrodes metals. Rain is slightly acidic and will slowly corrode steel.

An acid contains hydrogen ions. When an acid and a metal react together, hydrogen gas is given off. Magnesium and sulphuric acid react together vigorously.

An **alkali** is a substance which contains hydroxide ions made up of one oxygen atom and one hydrogen atom. Some alkalis such as sodium hydroxide and ammonium hydroxide are used in cleaning products for removing grease.

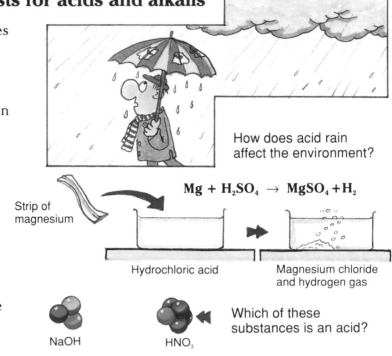

How does acid rain affect the environment?

Strip of magnesium

$$Mg + H_2SO_4 \rightarrow MgSO_4 + H_2$$

Hydrochloric acid

Magnesium chloride and hydrogen gas

NaOH

HNO$_3$

Which of these substances is an acid?

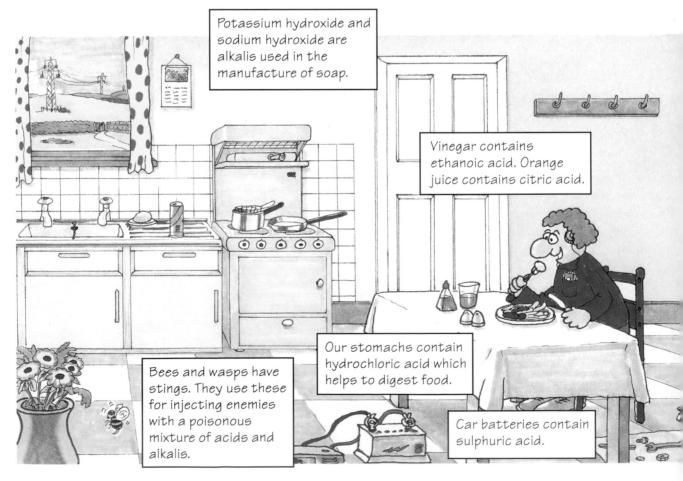

Potassium hydroxide and sodium hydroxide are alkalis used in the manufacture of soap.

Vinegar contains ethanoic acid. Orange juice contains citric acid.

Our stomachs contain hydrochloric acid which helps to digest food.

Bees and wasps have stings. They use these for injecting enemies with a poisonous mixture of acids and alkalis.

Car batteries contain sulphuric acid.

Both acids and alkalis contain hydrogen. However, acids give off hydrogen during a chemical reaction and alkalis take in hydrogen during a reaction. Different acids and alkalis have different strengths. A strong acid can give off a lot of hydrogen and a strong alkali can take in a lot of hydrogen. The **pH value** is a measure of the strength of an acid or alkali (p stands for power and H stands for hydrogen).

A substance with a pH value of 1 is a strong acid. A substance with a pH value of 14 is a strong alkali.

Chemists use a mixture of dyes called a Universal Indicator to determine the strength of acids and alkalis. A drop of the indicator is added to the liquid to be tested. The indicator changes to a colour which indicates the presence and strength of acid or alkali in the liquid.

Universal Indicator

pH value	1	2	3	4	5	6	7	8	9	10	11	12	13	14
Colour of Universal Indicator	← Red →			Pink	Orange	Yellow	Green	Green Blue	Blue	Blue Violet	← Violet →			
Substance	Acid						Neutral	Alkali						

Investigation

The chart below shows the strengths of some commonplace acids and alkalis. **Neutral** substances are neither acid nor alkali.

Which of these substances are acids and which are alkalis? Which is the strongest acid?

Substance	pH	Colour
Vinegar	4	Pink
Orange juice	6	Yellow
Distilled water	7	Green
Milk of magnesia	9	Blue
Sugar soap	12	Violet

Fizzy drinks are acidic and can damage teeth. If you wanted to compare the acid strengths of a selection of drinks, how would you do it?

Litmus paper

This is a simple indicator which tests for the presence of acids and alkalis. Acids turns blue litmus paper red and alkalis turns red litmus paper blue.

Litmus paper

Acid

Alkali

What effect do you think a neutral substance has on litmus paper?

SUMMARY

Acids react with metals and give off hydrogen gas.

Alkalis take in hydrogen during a reaction.

The pH scale is used to decribe the strength of acids and alkalis.

Indicators are used to show the presence of acids and alkalis.

NEUTRALIZATION

Reactions between acids and alkalis

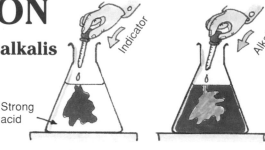

Strong acid

If a few drops of Universal Indicator are added to a strong acid, the liquid acid will turn red. If alkali is then added a few drops at a time, the liquid will turn pink and as more drops are added, it will eventually become neutral.

A **neutralization reaction** is one in which acids and alkalis react to form a neutral liquid. Hydrogen ions (H^+) in the acid react with hydroxide ions (OH^-) in the alkali to form water, which is neutral.

What colour will the liquid be when the acid and alkali have produced a neutral liquid?

Hydrogen ion(H^+)

Hydroxide ion(OH^-)

Water

What is the chemical formula for water?

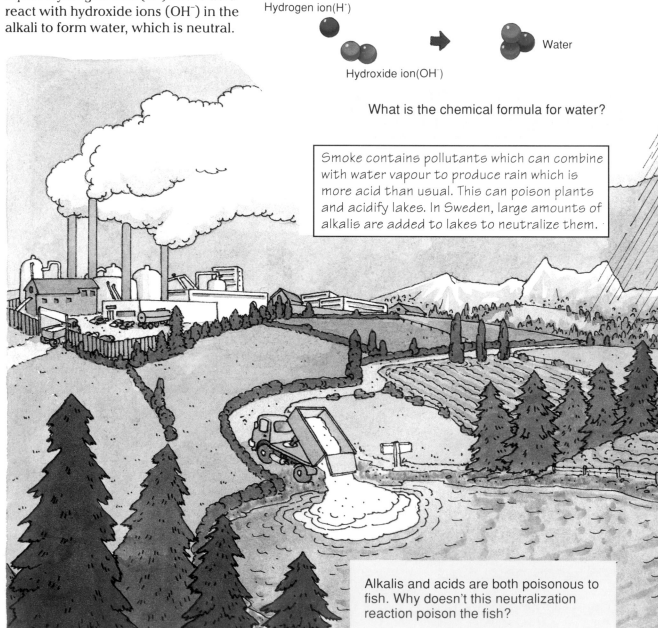

Smoke contains pollutants which can combine with water vapour to produce rain which is more acid than usual. This can poison plants and acidify lakes. In Sweden, large amounts of alkalis are added to lakes to neutralize them.

Alkalis and acids are both poisonous to fish. Why doesn't this neutralization reaction poison the fish?

Some acids are very strong. Strong acids have a large number of H^+ ions per unit volume. Sulphuric acid is a strong acid.

Some acids are weak. Weak acids have only a few H^+ ions per unit volume. Ethanoic acid is a weak acid. This is the acid found in vinegar.

A neutralization reaction is exothermic – it gives out heat.

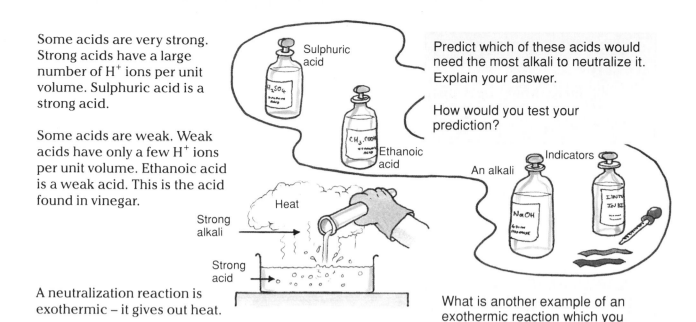

Sulphuric acid

H_2SO_4

Ethanoic acid

$CH_3.COOH$

Predict which of these acids would need the most alkali to neutralize it. Explain your answer.

How would you test your prediction?

An alkali

NaOH

Indicators

Heat

Strong alkali

Strong acid

What is another example of an exothermic reaction which you have seen in this book?

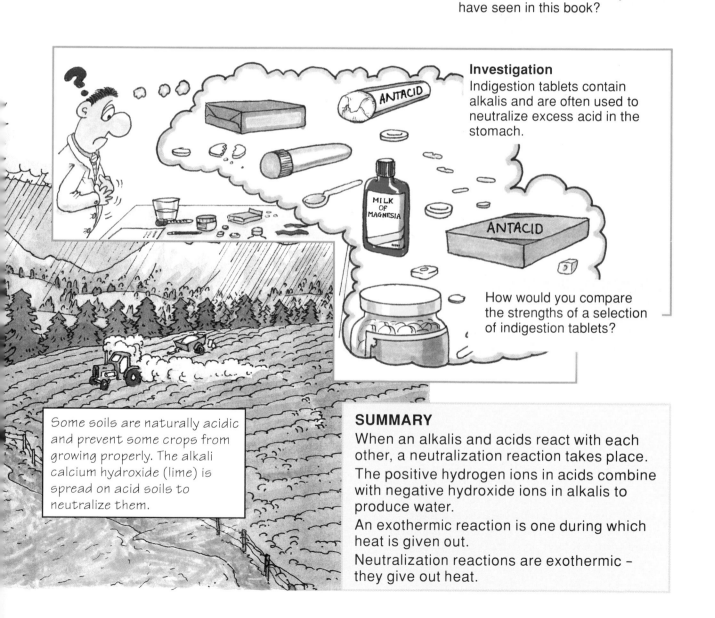

Investigation
Indigestion tablets contain alkalis and are often used to neutralize excess acid in the stomach.

ANTACID

MILK OF MAGNESIA

ANTACID

How would you compare the strengths of a selection of indigestion tablets?

Some soils are naturally acidic and prevent some crops from growing properly. The alkali calcium hydroxide (lime) is spread on acid soils to neutralize them.

SUMMARY
When an alkalis and acids react with each other, a neutralization reaction takes place.
The positive hydrogen ions in acids combine with negative hydroxide ions in alkalis to produce water.
An exothermic reaction is one during which heat is given out.
Neutralization reactions are exothermic – they give out heat.

SALTS
How salts are made and used

A **salt** is a substance formed when the hydrogen of an acid is replaced by a metal during a chemical reaction. Table salt (sodium chloride) is a well-known salt. There are thousands of other salts. Salts which dissolve in water are called **soluble salts.** There are five ways to make soluble salts.

Acids and alkalis react together to produce water and a salt. For example, sodium hydroxide reacts with hydrochloric acid to form sodium chloride (table salt) and water.

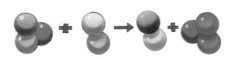

$$NaOH + HCl \rightarrow NaCl + H_2O$$

Which is the salt in this chemical reaction?

Acids react with metals to form a salt and hydrogen. For example, magnesium reacts with hydrochloric acid to produce magnesium chloride and hydrogen.

magnesium + hydrochloric → magnesium + hydrogen
             acid   chloride

How is this expressed as a chemical equation?

Heated acids react with metal oxides. For example, copper oxide reacts with sulphuric acid to produce copper sulphate and water.

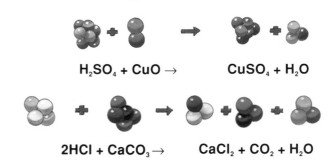

$$H_2SO_4 + CuO \rightarrow \qquad CuSO_4 + H_2O$$

Acids react with metal carbonates to produce a salt, carbon dioxide gas and water.
Metal carbonates are a group of substances which contain a metal, oxygen and carbon.

$$2HCl + CaCO_3 \rightarrow \qquad CaCl_2 + CO_2 + H_2O$$

Which is the metal carbonate in this chemical reaction?

Direct combination of two elements to form a salt can sometimes occur if at least one of the elements is very reactive.

iron filings + chlorine gas → ferric chloride
$$Fe + Cl_3 \rightarrow FeCl_3$$

Insoluble salts are made by mixing (in water) two soluble salts which each contain half of the required salt. This is called a **double decomposition** reaction. Here is an example. The downward pointing arrow shows which product is insoluble.

lead   + potassium → lead   + potassium
nitrate   iodide   iodide   nitrate
$$Pb(NO_3)_2 + 2KI \rightarrow PbI_2 \downarrow + KNO_3$$

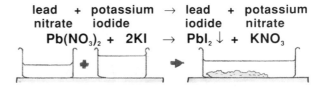

Is potassium nitrate soluble or insoluble?

Salts come from a wide variety of
sources and have many uses.

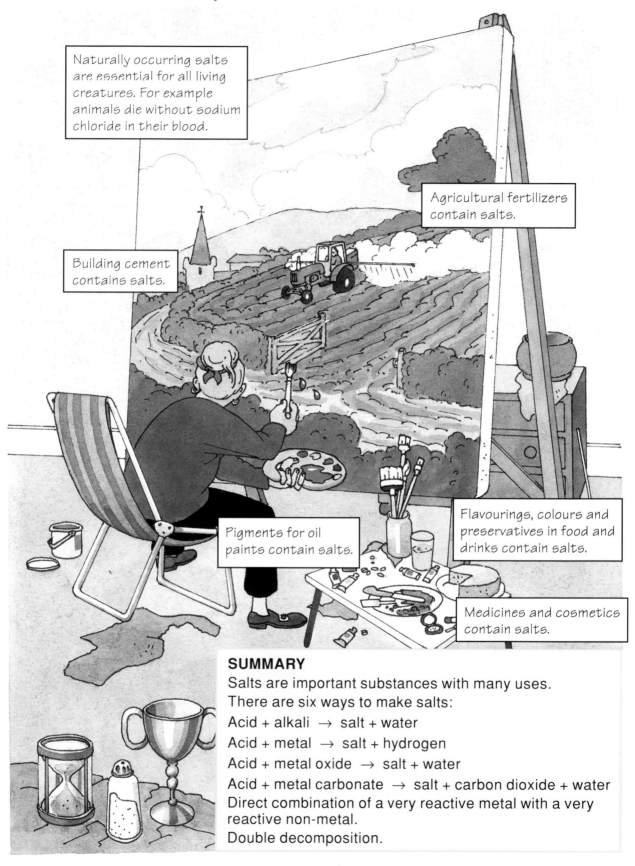

Naturally occurring salts
are essential for all living
creatures. For example
animals die without sodium
chloride in their blood.

Agricultural fertilizers
contain salts.

Building cement
contains salts.

Pigments for oil
paints contain salts.

Flavourings, colours and
preservatives in food and
drinks contain salts.

Medicines and cosmetics
contain salts.

SUMMARY
Salts are important substances with many uses.
There are six ways to make salts:
Acid + alkali $\rightarrow$ salt + water
Acid + metal $\rightarrow$ salt + hydrogen
Acid + metal oxide $\rightarrow$ salt + water
Acid + metal carbonate $\rightarrow$ salt + carbon dioxide + water
Direct combination of a very reactive metal with a very
reactive non-metal.
Double decomposition.

Key words appear in **bold** the first time
they occur in the text.

INDEX

Published by Heinemann Library,
an imprint of Heinemann Publishers (Oxford) Ltd,
Halley Court, Jordan Hill, Oxford, OX2 8EJ

OXFORD   LONDON   EDINBURGH
MADRID   PARIS   ATHENS   BOLOGNA
MELBOURNE   SYDNEY   AUCKLAND   SINGAPORE
TOKYO   IBADAN   NAIROBI   GABORONE   HARARE
PORTSMOUTH NH (USA)

© Lazy Summer Books Ltd. 1994
First published 1994
98 97 96 95 94
10 9 8 7 6 5 4 3 2 1
British Library Cataloguing Publication in Data
is available on request from the British Library.
ISBN 0-431-07601-4   (HB)
ISBN 0-431-07568-9   (PB)
Designed by Lazy Summer Books Ltd.
Illustrated by Lazy Summer Books Ltd.
Printed and bound in China